394·2

PUFFIN BOOKS

Why Does Santa Ride Around in a Sleigh?

Kay Woodward
once played one of
the ugly sisters in a
school pantomime of
Cinderella. A Christmas
Carol is one of her
favourite books. And
Christmas is one of
her favourite times
of year.

Why Does Santa Ride Around in a Sleigh?

... and other Christmas questions

Kay Woodward

Illustrated by Ian Cunliffe

PUFFIN

PUFFIN BOOKS

Published by the Penguin Group
Penguin Books Ltd, 80 Strand, London WC2R 0RL, England
Penguin Group (USA) Inc., 375 Hudson Street, New York, New York 10014, USA
Penguin Group (Canada), 90 Eglinton Avenue East, Suite 700, Toronto, Ontario, Canada M4P 2Y3
(a division of Pearson Penguin Canada Inc.)
Penguin Ireland, 25 St Stephen's Green, Dublin 2, Ireland (a division of Penguin Books Ltd)
Penguin Books (Australia) Ltd, 250 Camberwell Road, Camberwell, Victoria 3124, Australia
(a division of Pearson Australia Group Pty Ltd)
Penguin Books India Pvt Ltd, 11 Community Centre, Panchsheel Park, New Delhi – 110 017, India
Penguin Group (NZ), cnr Airborne and Rosedale Roads, Albany, Auckland 1310, New Zealand
(a division of Pearson New Zealand Ltd)
Penguin Books (South Africa) (Pty) Ltd, 24 Sturdee Avenue, Rosebank,
Johannesburg 2196, South Africa

Penguin Books Ltd, Registered Offices: 80 Strand, London WC2R 0RL, England

www.penguin.com

First published 2005
1

Text copyright © Kay Woodward, 2005
Illustrations copyright © Ian Cunliffe, 2005
All rights reserved

The moral right of the author and illustrator has been asserted

Set in Lemonade
Made and printed in England by Clays Ltd, St Ives plc

British Library Cataloguing in Publication Data
A CIP catalogue record for this book is available from the British Library

ISBN-13: 978-0-141-31872-1
ISBN-10: 0-141-31872-4

For Pippa

Contents

1

Why do we celebrate Christmas?

Every year, as it gets closer and closer to 25 December, marvellous things begin to happen. Bright lights are strung across busy streets. Decorations are fastened to walls and ceilings in homes and schools. Evergreen trees of all sizes appear in windows and in the middle of towns. Fairy lights glitter among the green branches and a shining star or an angel perches on the top of each tree. Leafy wreaths of holly and ivy are hung on front doors to welcome people inside. The delicious smell of Christmas cakes and mince pies wafts through kitchens. People sing carols in churches and in the frosty streets. Everyone begins to get very excited. Why. . .?

Because it's Christmas! Every year, millions of people around the world gather to celebrate the birth of the baby Jesus in Bethlehem, two thousand years ago. There are many different ways of celebrating. Perhaps you sing carols on Christmas Eve?

Maybe you leave out a drink of milk and a carrot for Father Christmas and his reindeer? But do you know why we do the same things year after year?

This book explains the reasons for and the stories behind many Christmas celebrations and traditions. Do you know why Boxing Day is called Boxing Day and why we kiss under the mistletoe? Why do we have Christmas trees? Turn the pages to find the answers ...

2

The Nativity and ancient festivals

❀—❀—❀—❀—❀—❀—❀—❀—❀

What does 'nativity' mean?

'Nativity' means 'birth'. But when people talk about the Nativity, they usually mean one particular birth – the baby Jesus's birth.

Just before school finishes for Christmas, lots of schools put on nativity plays. These plays tell the famous story of how Jesus was born. Luckily, there are so many characters in the Nativity story that there are enough parts for everyone.

There's Mary – Jesus's mother. Joseph is Mary's husband. When there was no room at his inn, the innkeeper let Mary and Joseph stay in his stable. There are the shepherds, who were told of Jesus's birth by the angel Gabriel. The three wise men came to visit the baby Jesus to bring presents. And don't forget all the animals in the stable!

What is a manger?

When they are born, most babies sleep in a cot, a crib or a basket. They are covered with blankets to keep them warm and snug. But, in the story of the Nativity, there were no cots or cribs in the stable where Jesus was born. Mary and Joseph had to find somewhere else for Him to sleep.

The manger – a long, narrow container that horses and cattle can eat from – was perfect! And, instead of blankets, the baby Jesus was kept warm with bundles of soft hay. Here are the first words from the Christmas carol 'Away in a Manger' . . .

Away in a manger, no crib for a bed,
The little Lord Jesus lay down His sweet head.
The stars in the bright sky looked down where He lay,
The little Lord Jesus, asleep on the hay.

Who were the three wise men?

In the story of the Nativity, many people travelled to Bethlehem to visit the baby Jesus. The most famous of these were the visitors who travelled on camels from the East – the three wise men. (There may have been more or there may have been fewer, but no one is really sure.) They have many other names too.

At Christmas, we sing about the three kings. Some people call them the three Magi. It is said that their actual names were Balthasar, Melchior and Caspar. Balthasar was a king of Arabia, Melchior was a king of Persia and Caspar was a king of India.

The three wise men didn't use a map to find the stable. Instead, they followed a bright star that appeared in the sky above Bethlehem when Jesus was born.
They brought with them very special gifts ...

What are gold, frankincense and myrrh?

These are the gifts that the three wise men gave to the baby Jesus. But they don't sound like presents that people usually give to babies. So what exactly are they?

The first part of this question has a very easy answer. Gold is a precious yellow metal that is found beneath the Earth's surface. It costs lots of money and is often made into beautiful jewellery and other shiny objects. Melchior brought a gift of gold to Bethlehem. This was a precious gift that someone as special as Jesus deserved.

Frankincense is the sticky juice that comes from the trunk of the *Boswellia* tree. It has a lovely sweet smell and it is sometimes burnt during religious ceremonies. Long ago, many people used it as a medicine. At the time of the Nativity, frankincense was in demand – and very expensive. It cost as much as gold and precious gems. It was Balthasar that brought frankincense to the stable.

Like frankincense, myrrh also oozes from the bark of a tree – the *Commiphora*. It can be burnt to give off a pleasant smell and is still used in some perfumes and medicines. Once again, it used to cost a lot of money. This was the gift that Caspar brought from the East to give to Jesus.

All three of the gifts were very special – they were given by kings and were fit for a king.

Why do we display models of the Nativity scene?

The Nativity scene, or crèche, was made famous by St Francis of Assisi – the patron saint of animals and the environment. On Christmas Eve 1223, he was visiting the town of Greccio, Italy.

He realized that the church wouldn't be big enough to hold all the people who would attend Midnight Mass, so instead he decided to make a life-sized Nativity scene in the town square.

St Francis filled a manger with hay and placed a doll on top. This would be the baby Jesus. Then he added statues of Mary and Joseph. As a finishing touch, he borrowed an ox and an ass from a local farmer. That night at midnight, crowds of people came to see the Nativity and to sing carols.

Today, Nativity scenes are usually *much* smaller!

When did the Nativity take place?

No one is sure exactly when Jesus was born. However, modern astronomers have studied star charts and calculated that a number of extra-bright stars appeared between 6 BC and 4 BC.

Any one of these stars might have been the star of Bethlehem that the wise men followed. Many people think it most likely that Jesus was born in March, 6 BC. So why is Jesus's birthday celebrated on 25 December? It's all to do with a totally different festival that took place on that day ...

The shortest day of the year is known as the winter solstice. This is when many people celebrate the fact that summer is on its way. In AD 274, the winter solstice fell on 25 December. Roman emperor Aurelian named this date 'The festival of the birth of the invincible sun' to celebrate the coming of light into the world.

Until the fourth century AD, Christmas was celebrated at different times of the year. But Pope Julius I wasn't happy with this. He thought that there should be a special day for Christmas – the same day every year.

In AD 320, Pope Julius decided that it would be a good idea if we celebrated Christmas on the same day as the winter solstice. His plan worked. For millions of people, Christmas Day is on 25 December and is now the most important day of the whole year.

What does 'Yule' mean?

Yule is the ancient word for the festival of
the winter solstice. In countries to the far
north, such as Sweden and Iceland, winters
are long and hard. In midwinter, there are
very few hours of daylight. Their winter-
solstice festival celebrates the fact that
the days are now beginning to grow longer
and that summer is coming.

The festival of Yule, also known as Yuletide,
lasted for twelve days. And a very special
part of the celebrations was the burning of
the yule log. This was dragged from nearby
woods and lit on the first day of Yule. To
ward off evil and guarantee luck for the following year, the log had to burn non-stop
until just a pile of ash and cinders remained.
Sometimes, a small piece of the burnt log was
kept until the following Yule. Then it was
used as kindling to light the next yule log.

As Yule and Christmas happened at the same
time, the traditions have crossed over. In
many European countries we sing hymns
about 'Yule' and eat delicious yule-log cakes.
For example, Portugal still has many yule-log

customs. The remains of the yule log are kept until the thunderstorm season later in the year. The ashes are then burnt with pinecones. It is said that the smoke from a yule log wards off lightning.

In some Portuguese village churches, a yule log is burnt so that the poor can keep themselves warm during the cold, wintry weather.

A scrummy yule log

The Victorians first had the idea of making a yule log that could be eaten. It's the easiest type of Christmas cake to put together. You don't even need to bake it in the oven!

What you need:

Two chocolate Swiss-roll cakes
100g soft butter
175g icing sugar
25g cocoa powder
A silver tray or patterned plate
Extra icing sugar for sprinkling
A Christmassy cake decoration or two
An adult to help you

what you do:

1. Sieve the icing sugar and the cocoa powder into a mixing bowl. Add the butter.

2. Mix the icing sugar, cocoa and butter together. This might take a few minutes. The mixture should be light and fluffy by the time you've finished.

3. Put one Swiss roll in the middle of the tray. This is going to be the yule log.

4. Ask your adult to cut the other Swiss roll into two – the ends should be diagonal, not straight. One piece should be bigger than the other. These are going to be the branches.

5. Carefully place your Swiss roll branches at the sides of the yule log. To make sure that they don't move, stick them on using the chocolate mixture.

6. Now for the fun part . . . Spread the rest of your mixture over the whole yule log and branches. Don't stop until it's totally covered.

7. Using a fork, make long marks on the
    finished chocolate icing.

8. Pop a Christmas-cake decoration on
    top. Then use a sieve to sprinkle a little
    icing sugar over the yule log.

Have a
delicious
Christmas!

3

Advent calendars and Christmas cards

What is Advent?

Advent is the name given to the days leading up to Christmas. It begins on the Sunday that is nearest to 30 November and ends on 24 December – Christmas Eve.

In many countries, the coming of Christmas is marked by the lighting of five Advent candles. These are placed in a leafy wreath, then one candle is lit on each Sunday of Advent and the final candle on Christmas Day.

Advent calendars are an exciting way to count down to Christmas. There are twenty-four doors – one to open on each day of December up to Christmas Eve.

The first advent calendar was made in
Germany in 1851 – with candles instead of
doors. It was over a hundred years later
before delicious chocolate-filled advent
calendars were first produced. Mmmm ...

Who made the first Christmas card?

In the UK, Christmas cards were first sold in
1843 – three years after the first stamp was
issued. Designed by London artist John
Calcott Horsley and sold by rich businessman Sir
Henry Cole, there were only a thousand
copies of the first card printed. They showed a
picture of people feeding the poor and
another picture of a Christmas party.

In 1870, Christmas cards became much more
popular. The Post Office introduced a new
cheaper stamp, which could be used to send
unsealed envelopes. Then, new printing
methods meant that cards were cheaper
too. Sales rocketed!

Christmas fact
The very first charity card was sent in 1949
– all profits went to UNICEF (the United
Nations Children's Fund). The picture on the
card was drawn by a seven-year-old girl.

Why do robins often appear on Christmas cards?

Every year, millions of Christmas cards are decorated with pictures of a tiny brown bird with a red chest – the robin. But even though the robin has become a Christmas symbol, it actually has very little to do with Christmas. Instead, it is so famous because of the Victorian postal service!

In the nineteenth century, postmen wore bright red uniforms and soon became known as robins or redbreasts. Some of the very first Christmas cards showed pictures of postmen delivering letters. And, before long, actual robin redbreasts began to appear on cards in place of the postmen. Over 150 years later, the robin is still as popular.

Christmas fact
The robin is the UK's national bird.

How many Christmas cards are sent?

Millions of people send Christmas cards to their friends and family every year. This creates sackloads of extra work for postal services around the world. Lots of temporary postal workers have to be hired to deliver the extra mail.

In 1822, the postmaster in Washington, DC, USA, became very worried about all the extra Christmas mail. So many people were sending letters and home-made cards at Christmas time that he had to hire sixteen extra staff to deliver them. The postmaster had a rather grumpy idea for dealing with his problem. He wanted a law that would limit the number of cards each person could send!

Luckily the law was never passed and people continue to send as many Christmas cards as they like.

4
Christmas customs, old and new

Who invented the most Christmas customs?

Some Christmas traditions, such as holly, ivy and mistletoe, date back thousands of years. Others, such as flashing fairy lights and Christmas pop songs, were invented in the twentieth century. But many Christmas customs were made popular by the Victorians – people who lived in Britain between 1837 and 1901.

Two of the most Christmassy Victorian inventions were the Christmas card and the Christmas cracker. The Victorians also liked to decorate their houses, especially with the Christmas tree, which was brought to Britain by Prince Albert, Queen Victoria's German husband.

Christmas fact

One of the most well-known Christmas stories ever was written by the famous Victorian Charles Dickens. *A Christmas Carol* tells the story of the mean, bad-tempered Ebenezer Scrooge, who hates the festive season and all it stands for. Whenever anyone mentions Christmas, Scrooge mutters his famous words – *'Bah humbug!'* Then, one snowy Christmas Eve, three spooky ghosts try to change Scrooge's mind. To find out if they succeed, you'll have to read the book!

Why do we kiss under the mistletoe?

Thousands of years ago, the mistletoe plant was worshipped by many ancient peoples, who believed that it had magical powers. It was also said to heal wounds. Mistletoe was so special that it had to be cut with a sickle – a sharp tool – made of gold!

Mistletoe ripens in December, which may be why it became associated with Christmas. In olden times, many people hung mistletoe in

their homes to protect themselves from evil spirits and to bring good luck. And, when enemies met underneath its white berries, they had to make friends until the following day.

In the eighteenth century, a kiss became a promise to marry. It may be that those who kissed under the mistletoe were sealing their promise in an extra-magical place.

Where does mistletoe grow?

Mistletoe is found in woods and forests in Europe, Asia and North America. There are over a thousand different types of mistletoe, but the most common is a plant with greenish-yellow leaves and white berries. (You or your pets must never eat these white berries, as they can be poisonous to humans and animals.)

Mistletoe can often be found growing on other plants or trees. It sends its roots deep into their branches, taking food from them in order to grow.

However, mistletoe also provides food and nesting sites for many birds. Blackbirds, thrushes, robins and pigeons eat mistletoe berries. Hawks and owls often nest among their leaves. The name 'mistletoe' may come from the missel thrush, a type of English garden bird.

Why do we pull Christmas crackers?

People have been pulling crackers since Christmas 1846. Their inventor, Tom Smith, got the idea while on holiday in Paris. When he spotted French sweets, he was very impressed. Each one was twisted into a piece of paper to keep it clean. At this time, British sweets were sold loose and unwrapped.

Tom brought the idea back to England, selling his wrapped sweets at Christmas. Then he had the idea of making a special type of sweet for Valentine's Day. This time, he put a romantic message inside too. But soon other confectioners were making special sweets like Tom. How could he make sure his sweets were different from everyone else's?

22

One evening, Tom was listening to logs crackling on his fire and had his best idea yet. He would make his sweet wrappers crack when they were opened!

They were a tremendous success, but Tom still wasn't happy. He had to make sure that his crackers were better than the rest.

After thinking long and hard, Tom decided to wrap a small present inside his cracker, instead of a sweet. His son Walter had the idea of putting a paper hat inside. The cracker had been invented – what a *cracking* idea!

Christmas fact

By 1900, Tom Smith had sold over thirteen million crackers! The Tom Smith company still makes christmas crackers today.

Christmas fact

crackers bang when two small strips of paper coated with a small amount of gunpowder are pulled apart.

Why do cracker jokes make people groan?

Cracker jokes make people groan because they are so *bad!* Christmas-cracker makers have tried putting better jokes inside their crackers, but people actually prefer dreadful jokes. They like to groan ... with laughter! Here are some of the very worst Christmas-cracker jokes!

WHY DOES SANTA LIKE TO WORK IN HIS GARDEN?
BECAUSE HE LIKES TO HOE, HOE, HOE!

WHAT DO YOU CALL A REINDEER WITH EARMUFFS ON?
ANYTHING YOU LIKE - HE CAN'T HEAR YOU

WHAT DO YOU GET IF YOU CROSS FATHER CHRISTMAS WITH A DUCK?
A CHRISTMAS QUACKER!

WHO PULLS FATHER CHRISTMAS'S SLEIGH WHEN THE WEATHER IS SHOWERY?
RAINDEER

WHAT MAKE A TINKLING SOUND WHEN
THEY COME THROUGH FATHER
CHRISTMAS'S LETTERBOX?
JINGLE BILLS

WHICH WAS THE CHEEKIEST REINDEER?
RUDE-OLPH

WHAT DO YOU CALL A COUNTRY WHERE REINDEER
RUN ROUND AND ROUND IN CIRCLES?
LAPLAND

What is Midnight Mass?

In the Christian church, it is traditional to
attend a special mass on Christmas Eve. This
mass usually takes place around twelve
o'clock at night and is called Midnight Mass.

At Midnight Mass, there are special readings,
communion, a sermon, prayers and lots of
carol singing! The mass may take place at
this time because midnight is the very
beginning of Christmas Day. Or it may be
because of the Nativity story, which

suggests that the baby Jesus was born at night. Shepherds in the fields heard the good news from the angel Gabriel. Here are the first few words from the carol that tells their story ...

While shepherds watched their flocks by night,
All seated on the ground,
The angel of the Lord came down,
And glory shone around.

Where does the word 'carol' come from?

The word 'carol' may come from the Greek word *'choraulein'*. This was a dance performed with flute music. In England, 'carol' became the word for a dance where everyone danced in a ring, while singing at the same time. As time passed, the meaning of 'carol' changed so that the word only meant singing.

Carols were once sung all year round, but over the years they became associated only with Christmas.

Christmas fact

Phillips Brooks was an American pastor who went on a journey to Bethlehem in 1865. When he returned home, he was inspired so much by what he'd seen that he wrote the words to one of the most famous carols – 'O Little Town of Bethlehem'. Lewis Redner, who played the organ in Brooks's church, wrote the music three years later.

Why do people go carol singing?

The tradition of carol singing dates back hundreds of years to the very old English custom of wassailing.

The word 'wassail' comes from the Old Norse phrase *'ves heilll'*, meaning 'to be in good health'. On Christmas Eve or Twelfth Night, people used to visit their friends and neighbours to wish each other a long and healthy life. Merrymakers went from door to door, drinking a toast from a wassail bowl or cup in each home.

Eventually, wassailing became carol singing. In the days before Christmas, groups of

carollers still go from house to house,
entertaining people as they go. If they are
lucky, they might be asked inside, or even
given mince pies to keep them warm. Many
carol singers give any money they collect
to charity.

When were the first carols sung?

A carol is a religious song or popular hymn
that is sung at Christmas. The tradition
dates back hundreds of years – at least as
far back as 1521, when the first English col-
lection of carols was published.

Since that time, hundreds of carols have been written. Some have been forgotten, but many remain popular, centuries after they were first sung. Many carols we sing today were written in the nineteenth century. Here are just a few ...

1818 – 'Silent Night'
1843 – 'O Come All Ye Faithful'
1848 – 'Once in Royal David's City'
1857 – 'We Three Kings of Orient Are'
1868 – 'O Little Town of Bethlehem'
1883 – 'Away in a Manger'

Which is *your* favourite carol?

What does 'Noel' mean?

'Noel' is a word that is often said or sung at Christmas. You may have heard it in this carol:

The first Noel the angel did say
Was to certain poor shepherds
*   in fields as they lay;*

In fields where they lay
tending their sheep,
On a cold winter's night
that was so deep.

Noel, Noel, Noel, Noel,
Born is the King of Israel.

In the story of the Nativity, the angel visited
the shepherds in the fields to tell them the
good news of Jesus's birth.

The French way of saying 'good news' is
'*les bonnes nouvelles*'. And this is where the
word 'Noel' comes from. In France, 'Noel'
became the word for Christmas.

How did the carol 'Silent Night' get its name?

On Christmas Eve in 1818, an Austrian priest
named Joseph Mohr was given some bad
news. He was told that his church organ was
broken. Even worse, it could not possibly be
repaired by midnight, in time for Midnight Mass.
Joseph was very upset – he simply couldn't

bear the thought of Christmas without music. So he decided to do something about it. Grabbing a pen and paper, he set about composing a brand-new Christmas carol – one that could be sung by a choir accompanied by a guitar.

By midnight, the carol was finished and the choir was ready. Slowly, quietly, the words of *Stille Nacht* began to ring through the small Austrian church.

When it was later translated into English, this carol became 'Silent Night'.

Was there really a Good King Wenceslas?

Good King Wenceslas really *did* exist. There were many kings with this name, but the one who stars in the well-known carol was born in around AD 907 near Prague (now in the Czech Republic).

Wenceslas I was raised by his loving grandmother. And, when he was old enough to be king, he tried to follow her example. He wanted to be a good leader and wanted to do good deeds.

But he had enemies – the German king Henry I the Fowler invaded in AD 929. Wenceslas didn't want war and surrendered. This angered many people, including his own brother Bolesav, who killed Wenceslas on his way to church.

After stories of miracles taking place near Wenceslas's tomb, the good king was made a saint. Nearly a thousand years later, a Christmas carol was written about the king who tried to do good.

Good King Wenceslas

Good King Wenceslas looked out
On the Feast of Stephen,
When the snow lay round about,
Deep and crisp and even;
Brightly shone the moon that night,
Tho' the frost was cruel,
When a poor man came in sight,
Gath'ring winter fuel.

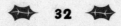

'Hither, page, and stand by me,
If thou know'st it, telling,
Yonder peasant, who is he?
Where and what his dwelling?'
'Sire, he lives a good league hence,
Underneath the mountain,
Right against the forest fence,
By Saint Agnes' fountain.'

'Bring me flesh, and bring me wine,
Bring me pine logs hither:
Thou and I will see him dine,
When we bear them thither.'
Page and monarch, forth they went,
Forth they went together;
Through the rude wind's wild lament
And the bitter weather.

'Sire, the night is darker now,
And the wind blows stronger;
Fails my heart, I know not how,
I can go no longer.'
'Mark my footsteps, good my page;
Tread thou in them boldly;
Thou shalt find the winter's rage
Freeze thy blood less coldly.'

In his master's steps he trod,
Where the snow lay dinted;
Heat was in the very sod
Which the saint had printed.
Therefore, Christian men, be sure,
Wealth or rank possessing,
Ye who now will bless the poor,
Shall yourselves find blessing.

When is the Feast of Stephen?

In the Christmas carol 'Good King Wenceslas', the king looks out 'on the Feast of Stephen'. But when is this?

Children from Ireland, Italy and many other countries will know the answer at once – St Stephen's Day is celebrated on 26 December, the day also known as Boxing Day. St Stephen was the first Christian martyr – a person who is killed for their religious beliefs. He was famous for looking after the poor.

In 1871, Boxing Day was made an official bank holiday in England, Wales and Ireland.

As Christmas Day was already a holiday, this gave people more time to travel long distances. This may be why traditionally people see family and friends at Christmas.

5
All that glitters – Christmas decorations

Who made the first Christmas decorations?

Every Christmas, supermarkets and gift shops sell a glittering array of decorations. There are colourful baubles and tiny trinkets to hang on the tree. There are paper garlands and strings of tinsel to drape around the house. There are even battery-powered Christmas trees and Father Christmases that sing when someone claps.

These decorations and ornaments are made in factories around the world, but early decorations were all home-made. People used to decorate their trees with paper flowers, apples, biscuits and sweets. Glass decorations were first made in the 1860s, in Lauscha, Germany. They were very popular and flew off the shelves as fast as they could be produced.

Decorations are still made in Lauscha today.

How do you 'deck the halls'?

Have you heard the Christmas carol that begins like this ...?

Deck the halls with boughs of holly,
Fa-la-la-la-la, la-la-la-la.
'Tis the season to be jolly,
Fa-la-la-la-la, la-la-la-la.

'Deck' is an old-fashioned word for 'decorate', so this carol is all about putting up Christmas decorations of holly.

Why not make your own Christmas decorations? They're easy to make and look fantastically festive.

A Christmas lantern

what you need:

An A4 or A3 sheet of coloured card
Scissors
Sticky tape

what you do:

1. Fold the card in half.
2. Cut slits three-quarters of the way across the folded card all the way down. All the slits should be the same length.
3. Unfold the card, then fold it down the other way and fix the ends together with sticky tape.
4. You can now stand your lamp on a table or hang it from the ceiling.

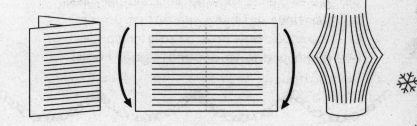

To make your lantern look extra-special, why not decorate the card with glitter before you start? Make sure you decorate the right side, though – this is the side of the card that faces outwards when it is folded in half.

Paper chains

These are the easiest Christmas decorations ever! All you need are strips of coloured paper and glue.

1. Take a strip, curl it round, then glue the two ends together to make a circle.
2. Now loop another strip through the middle of the circle. Make sure it's a different colour to the first one. Glue the two ends together into another circle.
3. Continue until you run out of paper.
4. You should now have a really long paper chain, ready to decorate your room!

Why are holly and ivy used as decorations at Christmas?

During the winter solstice people used to decorate their houses with evergreen leaves like holly, ivy and mistletoe. These plants were said to be lucky and also reminded everyone that spring was on its way.

When Christmas began to be celebrated, some of the old traditions became mixed up with the new ones. People continued to hang leafy decorations in December, although these were now linked with the story of Jesus rather than festivals of long ago.

Why do people hang a wreath on their front door?

At Christmas, many people decorate their front doors with wreaths. These can be made of woven evergreen leaves, such as fir, holly and ivy. Pinecones and ribbons add a festive finishing touch.

This tradition dates back two thousand years to Roman times. At New Year, the Romans used to exchange branches of evergreens as a way of wishing each other good health for the coming year. As more branches were collected, they were woven together to form a wreath, which was displayed on the front door.

Today, when people have often travelled from both near and far to visit family and friends, a wreath is the perfect way to welcome them.

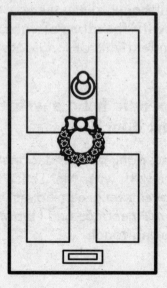

6

Christmas tree facts revealed

Why do we have Christmas trees?

People worshipped evergreen trees long before the Nativity took place. Because they were green all year round, they were seen as a symbol of life. Trees were first linked with Christmas in Germany during the sixteenth century. As fairy lights hadn't been invented, trees – both inside the house and out – were decorated with roses, apples and coloured paper.

In Austria and Germany during the seventeenth and eight-eenth centuries, there was a very strange Christmas-tree tradition ... The tops of fir and pine trees were cut off and then hung from the ceiling –

upside down! These topsy-turvy trees were decorated with strips of red paper, apples and nuts.

Christmas fact
In Australia, many people decorate gum trees instead of pine trees.

When did Christmas trees become popular?

It was Queen Victoria's husband, Prince Albert, who helped to make Christmas trees so popular. In 1834, he brought a Christmas tree to Windsor Castle. After this, the royal family decorated a tree every year.

Each one of Victoria and Albert's trees was magnificent. The branches groaned with candles, ribbons, cakes, gingerbread and other Christmas treats. Around the bottom of the tree, dolls, sweets and other presents were piled. And on the very top, there perched a small angel.

Christmas fact
Most people buy their Christmas trees. But did you know that you can hire a Christmas tree for the festive season? They are planted in pots, so that they can be returned to the shop and replanted after Christmas.

Why do people put a star or an angel on the top of the tree?

These traditions are based on the story of the Nativity. When Jesus was born, it is said, a star appeared above the stable in which He lay. It became known as the Star of Bethlehem. This is what the star on top of a Christmas tree represents.

The angel Gabriel told everyone the good news of Jesus's birth, appearing before the shepherds in the fields. The angel is another symbol of the Nativity that is represented as a Christmas-tree decoration.

Christmas fact
If Christmas trees are left to grow naturally, they do not have such a neat triangular shape. They have to be clipped each spring to encourage them to grow in this way.

Why do we have tinsel?

Tinsel was invented in Germany in 1610. The very first tinsel was a twinkling, glittering decoration made of real silver. Later, inventors tried to make cheaper tinsel using a mixture of lead and tin, but it was too heavy and too easy to break, so silver was used once more. Foil is now used to make shiny tinsel.

There is an old story that explains why we decorate Christmas trees with tinsel. Long ago, a widow was left to bring up her large family alone. They were very poor, but she worked hard to pay for a Christmas tree. Then, on Christmas Eve, spiders ruined her

surprise by covering the tree with cobwebs. It is said that when the Christ child saw the cobwebs, He turned the webs into shining silver.

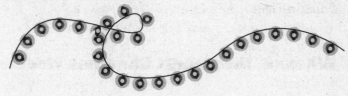

Who decided to put fairy lights on the Christmas tree?

No Christmas tree would be complete without a set of twinkling fairy lights. White or coloured, shining or flashing, they are the perfect finishing touch.

American Thomas Edison invented the electric light bulb in 1879 – and fairy lights weren't far behind. Just three years later, one of Edison's workmates had a set of electric lights made. That Christmas, Edward Johnson invited his friends and family to his home in New York City. There, he astounded and amazed them with his beautiful, glowing Christmas tree.

Christmas fact

Before fairy lights were invented, people used to decorate their Christmas trees with candles. This was very dangerous and often caused fires.

Where is the biggest Christmas tree?

Many countries around the world have an official Christmas tree that is displayed in a public place. In the USA, a giant *sequoia* (redwood tree) named the General Grant Tree grows in the King's Canyon National Park in California. It is over eighty metres tall and was named the national Christmas tree in 1925. This may be the biggest Christmas tree in the world.

Every Christmas, a large tree stands in Trafalgar Square in London. This is a gift from the people of Norway to thank the UK for their help during the Second World War. Each November, a Norwegian spruce is felled during a special ceremony, while children sing carols. It is then taken to London. The tree's lights are switched on in early December – they are never coloured, always white.

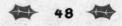

Where do Christmas trees come from?

Different types of spruce, pine and fir trees are grown all over the world specially to be used as Christmas trees.

In the UK alone, about six million trees are sold every year. The best-selling trees are Norway spruce, Scots and Lodgepole pine, and Noble and Nordmann fir. Christmas trees are grown throughout Scotland, the Lake District, the Peak District and many other parts of the UK.

For every Christmas tree that is felled, at least two seedlings are planted.

Christmas fact
The best way to stop a Christmas tree dropping its pine needles all over the carpet is to regularly top up its pot with water. Christmas trees need as much as 500 ml of water a day.

What happens to Christmas trees after Christmas?

When the decorations come down, it's time to say goodbye to the Christmas tree too. Some people keep their Christmas tree in the garden all year. Before Christmas, they replant the tree in a pot and bring it into the house. After Christmas, the tree can be put back into the garden.

Many fir trees have their roots chopped off before they are sold. These can't be planted again, but they can be taken to a recycling centre. Here, they are ground up into small pieces and left to rot until they become compost. This can be used to help other plants grow.

One of the most environmentally friendly Christmas trees is the artificial tree. This can be used over and over again and never has to be thrown away!

Why do we give Christmas presents?

Long ago, people used to give presents to each other on the shortest day of the year – the winter solstice. And, although Christmas began to be celebrated on 25 December during the fourth century, it was not until the nineteenth century that Christmas presents became really popular.

First, only rich people could afford to give them. Then, new factories were able to make things more quickly and more cheaply. This meant that poor people could afford to give presents too.

The tradition of Christmas presents may date back to the story of the three wise men. They travelled all the way to Bethlehem to give presents to the baby Jesus. These were the very first Christmas gifts.

7
Ho, Ho, Ho!
It's Father Christmas

Who is Father Christmas?

Father Christmas is the kindly old gentleman who helps to make Christmas special every year. He's easy to recognize. He has a white, bushy beard and fluffy white eyebrows. He has rosy round cheeks and a gentle smile. He always wears the same outfit – a red coat and trousers, with white, furry edges. A red hat with a white bobble and a furry rim perches on top of his head.

Father Christmas is a jolly fellow – he spends most of his time *ho-ho-ho*-ing. Even though Christmas Eve is his busiest night of the year, it's also the night that he has the most fun. Can you imagine how fantastic it must be to skim over the rooftops, making people smile wherever your sleigh lands ...?

Who is St Nicholas?

St Nicholas was born in Turkey over 1,700 years ago. He was bishop of the city of Myra and was well known for his good deeds, especially to children, to the poor, and to the unhappy. It is said that he performed many miracles, once bringing children back to life. Even the Romans couldn't keep him quiet – they captured him, but soon released him.

St Nicholas became the patron saint of many countries, cities and groups of people, including Russia and Greece, charities, sailors and children.

Many people believe that Father Christmas and St Nicholas are actually the same person ...

Christmas fact
St Nicholas's Day is celebrated on 6 December. In the Netherlands and many other countries, this is the day that children receive their Christmas presents.

Why do we hang up stockings on Christmas Eve?

Children hang up stockings on Christmas Eve because of St Nicholas. An old story tells of three girls who were very poor and very sad. Because they had no money, no one would marry them. And if no one married them, they would become poorer still and have to live on the streets.

St Nicholas heard of the three girls and decided to help them. One night, he threw three gold coins down their chimney. These coins would have fallen into the fire had the three girls not hung up their stockings to dry. Instead, the coins fell into the stockings and the girls were no longer poor or sad.

Christmas fact
A gift of an orange or a tangerine in a Christmas stocking is said to represent the gold coin left by St Nicholas.

Why is Father Christmas also called Santa Claus?

Father Christmas has many different names around the world, but one of the most popular is Santa Claus. This name comes from the Netherlands.

In the sixteenth century, Dutch children used to leave their clogs near the fireplace on 6 December (St Nicholas's Day). If they were lucky, St Nicholas would leave a treat inside these wooden shoes.

In the Netherlands, St Nicholas was spelt *Sint Nikolaas*. This became *Sinterklaas*. When Dutch settlers travelled to America, they took the name with them to New Amsterdam (now New York City). Finally, St Nicholas became Santa Claus!

Christmas fact
In Ireland, Santa Claus is also known as 'Santy'.

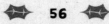

Does Father Christmas have any other names?

You might think that Father Christmas has more than enough names already, but he has yet more! Here are just a few ...

Babbo Natale – Italy
Joulupukki – Finland
På Norsk – Norway
Papá Noel – Spain
Père Noël – France and Canada
San Nicolás – Mexico
Santa no ojisan – Japan

He is also known as St Nick, which is short for St Nicholas.

Christmas fact
In some parts of Russia, a jolly old man called Grandfather Frost delivers presents at New Year instead of Christmas. He looks a little like Father Christmas, but often wears blue instead of red.

Does Father Christmas deliver presents to everyone?

Father Christmas delivers presents to all the children that believe in him. (It also helps to write him a letter.) But in some parts of the world, other people bring the presents.

In Scandinavia, Christmas gnomes visit. In Germany, the *Christkind* – a girl wearing a crown of flickering candles – delivers presents. Here are some other festive visitors ...

The Three Kings

In Spain and South America, the Three Kings deliver presents on 6 January, which is known as Three Kings' Day. This is the day that the three wise men brought gifts to the baby Jesus in the Nativity story.

Babouschka

In some parts of Russia, Babouschka brings presents for children. It is said that on their way to Bethlehem, the three wise men stayed at Babouschka's house. She fed them and gave them a bed for the night. The next day, the wise men asked Babouschka to follow

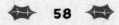

the star with them, but she refused. She was too busy. She didn't have time to travel to see the new baby. So she stayed at home.

The next day, Babouschka felt sad. She wished she'd gone to Bethlehem. So she gathered up a basket of toys and followed the three wise men. But when she reached the stable, it was empty.

It is said that Babouschka still travels the world, leaving gifts beside sleeping children, just in case one of them is the one she's searching for.

La Befana

A kindly old witch called La Befana delivers presents to the children of Italy. She wears tattered old clothes, flies on a broomstick and visits on 6 January every year. Her story is very like Babouschka's sad tale.

What are naughty children supposed to get for Christmas?

If Father Christmas only brings presents to children who have been good, what does he leave the children who have misbehaved? Here are some clues ... They're lumpy, they're dirty and they're good for lighting fires. They're pieces of coal!

This tradition comes from Italy. It is said that the friendly old witch, *La Befana* flies around on her broomstick delivering presents. She leaves lumps of coal in children's Christmas stockings to remind them to be good all year round.

So, if you ever feel like being really naughty in December – don't. It's not worth the risk. The last thing you want to find in your stocking on Christmas Day is a lump of coal!

Christmas fact
In Italy, there is a type of sweet that looks like coal. Italian children (even good ones!) sometimes find this – instead of real coal – in their Christmas stocking.

Where does Father Christmas live?

No one knows exactly where Father Christmas lives. Many people believe that he lives at the North Pole. But the people of Lapland disagree – they say Father Christmas lives in their country instead.

Lapland is a very cold place where lots of reindeer live. It stretches across northern Norway, Sweden and Finland.

So how can you send Father Christmas a letter if you don't know his address? Don't worry! You can post a letter to the address on page 62. Or you can write to him in Lapland. But, every single letter that has *Father Christmas* or *Santa Claus* written on the envelope will reach him. He has magical ways of making sure that no letter is ever lost in the Christmas post ...

How do you contact Father Christmas?

It's quite easy to get in touch with Father Christmas. First, it's best to write a letter or an email. Of course, you won't forget to include a list of the presents that you would like Father Christmas to bring down the chimney for you. But that's not all.

How about asking if Father Christmas is well? And the reindeer? If he receives a nice, polite, chatty letter from you, Father Christmas will be far more likely to bring the presents on your list. And don't forget to tell him if you've been good or bad, because he does like to know these things ...

Father Christmas's postal address:
Father Christmas
The Grotto
North Pole

Father Christmas's email address:
santa@santaclaus.com

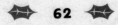

Who are Santa's little helpers?

Santa is the speediest present deliverer in the whole world. Every Christmas Eve, he whizzes over the rooftops, leaving gifts and making dreams come true. But not even Santa has the time to make and wrap all of these presents too.

Luckily, he has lots of little helpers to lend a hand – the elves! Here are the names of just six of the elves. There might be three more. There might be 300 more. Their numbers and their names are a closely guarded secret ...

Alabaster Snowball makes a careful note of who's been naughty and who's been nice during the year. He thinks it's a very good idea if children are nice.

Bushy Evergreen is in charge of making the toys. It's his job to make sure that every child receives exactly the right gift.

Pepper Ministix makes sure that no one knows where Santa lives. His job is to keep his lips very tightly shut and not give away *any* secrets at all. Not even the one about ... Shhhhhhh!

Shinny Upatree is Santa's best friend. He takes care of the other elves.

Sugarplum Mary is in charge of making chocolatey presents and other sweet gifts.

Wunorse Openslae has one of the most important jobs of all. He's the sleigh mechanic and reindeer keeper. Without him, the sleigh wouldn't fly, the reindeer wouldn't get treats and no one would receive any Christmas presents.

Why were letters to Father Christmas traditionally sent up the chimney?

In past times, most people had real fires burning in their fireplaces. Letters to Father Christmas would be sent up the chimney. (This was *always* done by an adult.) The best way to make sure that a letter whizzed right up the chimney, to be blown all the way to the North Pole, was to make sure that the door was open. This meant that there was a draught of air ready to blow the letter upwards on its way. Sometimes, letters were

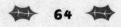

thrown on to a burning fire instead. The smoke would carry the Christmas wishes up the chimney to Father Christmas.

In Scotland, it was traditional to shout their Christmas requests up the chimney instead of writing a letter. This was called 'crying up the lum'.

Does everyone send letters to Father Christmas?

Father Christmas receives sacks and sacks of letters every single year from children all over the world. But in some countries it is not traditional to write to him.

Italian children have a very different custom. Instead, they write letters to their parents, telling them how much they love them. And, instead of being posted or sent up the chimney, this letter is put underneath their mum or dad's plate on Christmas Eve. After the evening meal has been eaten, the letters are read.

Christmas fact
In Italy, it is traditional to give your best friend a bag of lentils at Christmas. These are used to make lentil soup, which is said to bring good luck in the New Year.

What should you leave out for Father Christmas on Christmas Eve?

Delivering presents is tiring work – especially when you have as many presents to deliver as Father Christmas. It's also hungry and thirsty work. So, before you go to bed on Christmas Eve, it's very important that you leave out a snack.

Father Christmas's favourite treats are mince pies and Christmas cake, but anything will do. You might also want to leave a small glass of sherry or brandy to wash the food down. Or a glass of milk – rumour has it that the jolly Christmas visitor is very fond of this.

Whatever you do, don't forget to leave a snack for the reindeer.

After all, they're the ones pulling the sleigh – and you don't want them to run out of energy!

Why does Father Christmas come down the chimney?

In the winter, it is usually so cold that everyone keeps their windows tightly shut at night. At first, this created a problem for a certain special visitor in a red-and-white coat. How was he supposed to get into each house to deliver presents without waking anyone? He looked and looked and soon spotted that there was way to get inside a house that was never locked or shut – down the chimney!

If you haven't got a chimney, you're probably wondering how Father Christmas gets into your house. Well, the answer is … nobody knows, apart from Father Christmas himself. It's just one of those magical things about Christmas Eve.

Do animals get Christmas presents?

Of course they do! Father Christmas loves animals (especially reindeer) and makes sure that they get treats at Christmas too. He often leaves them new collars, toys or other Christmassy treats.

Pets sometimes get a little confused or overexcited at Christmas. If they have something new to play with or a treat to munch, they are far less likely to be upset by the rustling, tearing and crumpling of wrapping paper!

One thing that should never be put on your Christmas list is a pet. Every year, many pets are given as Christmas presents and, every New Year, many of these pets are taken to animal rescue centres because their new owners can't look after them.

Why does Father Christmas ride around in a sleigh?

A sleigh is by far the best way of delivering presents around the world. Father Christmas's sleigh is made of wood. This means that it is sturdy enough to carry huge sacks of gifts, but it is also light enough to be pulled through the air.

Underneath the sleigh there are long, smooth runners that act like skis. When Father Christmas touches down, the runners allow the sleigh to slide over snow, ice, frosty roofs and even sandy beaches.

Sleighs are usually pulled by horses or by reindeer. Because Father Christmas lives near the very top of the world, he prefers to use reindeer. They are used to the icy-cold weather. Father Christmas's reindeer are also very good at flying.

What are jingle bells?

Every time you see a sleigh, you'll also hear the beautiful tinkling sound of jingle bells.

These are tiny bells that are hung on the sleigh or the reindeer or horses that are pulling it. They warn people that a sleigh is coming – and they also sound very Christmassy!

You might have heard people sing about them in this song ...

Dashing through the snow,
In a one-horse open sleigh,
Through the fields we go,
Laughing all the way.
Bells on bobtail ring,
Making spirits bright,
What fun it is to ride and sing
A sleighing song tonight.

Jingle bells, jingle bells,
Jingle all the way,
Oh what fun it is to ride
In a one-horse open sleigh.

What is a reindeer?

A reindeer is a type of deer. Reindeer live in very cold places, such as the North Pole,

Lapland, Siberia, Canada and Alaska. They have beautiful thick fur to keep them warm. Their coats are usually white, grey, dark grey or brown.

Reindeer have wide hooves. These allow the animals to walk on snow or soft ground without sinking in. They can also use their hooves as spades – to dig in the snow for food.

Unlike every other type of deer, both male and female reindeer have antlers. They use these to fight or to protect their young from danger.

Christmas fact
All deer whether young, old, male or female, grow a new set of antlers every year.

What are the names of Father Christmas's reindeer?

Father Christmas needs eight strong reindeer to pull him through the night skies on Christmas Eve. (Otherwise, it would take him so long to travel around the world that you might not get your presents until Easter!) The names of the trusty reindeer are Dasher, Dancer, Prancer, Vixen, Comet, Cupid, Donder and Blitzen. If the names sound a little odd, that's probably because they are nearly two hundred years old.

A writer called Clement Clarke Moore gave the reindeer these names in his poem 'A Visit from St Nick'. This later became known as 'The Night before Christmas' (1822). And, just in case you haven't read it, here's the very first verse ...

'Twas the night before Christmas, when all
     through the house
Not a creature was stirring, not even a mouse.
The stockings were hung by the chimney with care,
In hopes that St Nicholas soon would be there ...

Christmas fact
Although some people believe that Father Christmas has a reindeer called Donner, he is called Donder in Clement Moore's original poem.

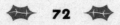

Did Rudolph the Red-nosed Reindeer really exist?

Rudolph the Red-nosed Reindeer was invented by American advertiser Robert L. May.

Robert worked for a store in Chicago owned by a man called Montgomery Ward. Montgomery liked to give his customers a treat. So in 1939, he decided that the store would give children a special Christmas booklet. And he asked Robert to write a Christmas story that could be printed in the booklet.

When he was younger, Robert had always been the odd one out. Children made fun of him because he was so small and laughed at him for being shy. This gave the grown-up Robert an idea. He would write a story about a reindeer who didn't fit in - a reindeer who was a little bit different from all the rest. This was Rudolph the Red-nosed Reindeer.

Rudolph's story was written in verse. Robert's own daughter loved it, but Montgomery wasn't so sure. Was a red-nosed reindeer a good idea?

To convince him, the author asked a friend to draw some pictures of Rudolph and his shiny nose. As soon as he saw them, the store owner was convinced. He printed and gave away millions of copies of the Rudolph booklet over the next few years.

Rudolph the Red-nosed Reindeer became the most famous of them all.

Christmas fact
Robert's brother-in-law, songwriter Johnny Marks, wrote the music and adapted the words for the 'Rudolph the Red-nosed Reindeer' song. It was a huge hit.

Why does Father Christmas dress in red and white?

Father Christmas has not always worn a red and white outfit. Very early pictures showed

him wearing a long brown robe and furs,
with a holly crown perched on his head.

In 1862, an American cartoonist called
Thomas Nast began to draw black and white
pictures of Father Christmas, getting many
of his ideas from Clement C. Moore's famous
poem – 'The Night before Christmas':

... He was dressed all in fur, from his head to his foot,
And his clothes were all tarnished with ashes and soot.
A bundle of toys he had flung on his back,
And he looked like a peddler just opening his pack.

His eyes – how they twinkled! his dimples, how merry!
His cheeks were like roses, his nose like a cherry!
His droll little mouth was drawn up like a bow,
And the beard on his chin was as white as the snow.

The stump of a pipe he held tight in his teeth,
And the smoke it encircled his head like a wreath.
He had a broad face and a little round belly,
That shook when he laughed, like a bowl full of jelly ...

In 1885, a printer from Boston called Louis Prang decided to add some colour. He chose a bright-red suit.

In 1931, artist Haddon Sundblom drew pictures of Father Christmas wearing red and white in the Coca-Cola Company's adverts. He still wears the same colours today.

What is Santa's grotto?

Father Christmas only delivers presents when people are fast asleep. (That's why it's no use trying to stay awake on Christmas Eve – you'll *never* see him then.) But, during the month of December, many children get the chance to see the famous old man in the red and white suit.

Santa's grotto is a magical place. You might find one in a shopping centre or a department store. Inside, there are glittering walls and decorations. There's also Father Christmas.

You might wonder how Father Christmas can visit lots of grottoes at the same time. This

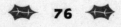

would be totally impossible, so he asks his best friends to dress up in red and white instead. But, not many people know that the real Father Christmas does visit *every single grotto* at some time during December. So ... when you visit Father Christmas in his grotto, he just might be the real one!

8

Tuck into Christmas food

Why do we eat mince pies?

Mince pies have been eaten at Christmas for 500 years. But the first mince pies were very different to those we eat today. They were much bigger and they were oval, not round. This long, narrow shape was meant to look like the manger from the Nativity scene. The pastry on top represented the clothes that the baby Jesus was wrapped in.

Mince pies are also said to represent Christ and his twelve disciples. This is because they used to contain twelve ingredients, plus minced mutton – the lamb is a symbol of Christ.

Mince pies are still one of the most popular Christmas treats – millions of them are eaten every year. To make the pies extra-Christmassy, some people now put a pastry star on top and sprinkle them with icing sugar.

Why are mince pies called mince pies when they don't have mince in them?

Mince pies are filled with a mysterious, dark gloopy mixture called mincemeat. But why is it called mincemeat? It doesn't have mince in it and neither does it contain any other sort of meat!

The truth is that, once, mincemeat *did* contain minced meat. Mince pies made with meat date back to Roman times and were even eaten a hundred years ago. Early recipes for mincemeat included lamb, pheasant and rabbit. Then raisins, apples and dried orange peel were added to the recipe. Soon, there was more fruit than meat. And, at the beginning of the twentieth century, mince pies became totally meat-free. They now contain a mixture of dried fruit.

Why do Christmas cakes have marzipan and icing on them?

Christmas cakes are decorated with marzipan and icing so that they look and taste delicious!

Marzipan is made from ground almonds. It is rolled out and then placed on to the cooked Christmas cake. As a fruit cake can be lumpy and bumpy, the marzipan makes a flatter surface for the icing to lie on. It also stops the icing becoming stained with any juices that might seep out of the cake. Icing is the perfect finishing touch – a sweet, white topping. This can be smoothed flat, or made into snowy peaks.

Christmas fact
Until Victorian times, Christmas cake was not decorated with marzipan or icing. It was just a plain old fruit cake.

Why do we eat Christmas pudding?

Long ago, people ate a special type of spiced porridge called frumenty. For the rich, this was a dish to eat with venison. But for the poor, who could not afford to make frumenty very often, it was a treat for special occasions such as Christmas.

Frumenty became plum porridge, which became the firm plum pudding or Christmas pudding that we now eat.

There are lots of different recipes for Christmas pudding, but most include dried fruit, mixed peel, nuts, apples, eggs and spices. Delicious!

Traditionally, Christmas puddings were always made on the nearest Sunday to 23 November. This day is known as Stir-up Sunday. It may seem a long time before 25 December, but it means that the pudding will be really sticky and tasty by Christmas Day.

On Stir-up Sunday, everyone in the family has a turn at stirring the ingredients for the pudding. But if you get the chance to stir a

pudding, there are two things that you must do. These are:

1. Make a wish.
2. Stir in a clockwise direction.
If you stir the other way, your wish won't come true!

Perhaps the most exciting tradition is that of setting light to the Christmas pudding. (This is always done by an adult.) First of all, the lights should be turned out. A small amount of brandy or rum is warmed in a saucepan. Then, the liquid is poured on to the pudding before being carefully set alight. *Ta-daaaaah!*

Why was there a sixpence in the Christmas pudding?

Did you know that three things used to be added to the Christmas pudding that could not be eaten? An old silver sixpence was once popped into the mixture. It was said that whoever found the coin would become rich. A ring was also added. Whoever found this would soon marry. The third object was a thimble. If you found this in your pudding, it was said that you would have a lucky life.

Today, some people still put a coin into their home-made pudding. A large coin is easier to spot. Remember to clean it first – if you drop a coin into a glass of cola, it will soon be nice and shiny. Most important of all, remember to tell everyone that there's a coin somewhere in the pudding!

Does everybody eat turkey at Christmas?

Turkey is very popular at Christmas, especially in the UK, Australia, USA and Belgium, but not everybody eats a traditional turkey dinner. Many people prefer goose, chicken or fish. Vegetarians enjoy a festive meat-free dish.

In Spain, the traditional meal is turkey and truffles – these are a rare and extra-special type of fungi a little like mushrooms. The Finnish eat a casserole of macaroni and vegetables with cooked ham or turkey. Many Brazilians eat chicken and rice.

Christmas fact
In Australia, the weather is so warm at
Christmas that many people eat their dinner
on the beach. Instead of being roasted,
their turkey is cooked on the barbecue!

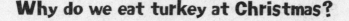

Why do we eat turkey at Christmas?

Long ago, before the Nativity, it was traditional to cook and serve a large joint of
meat in wintertime. It was hoped that this
would please the gods celebrated at the
winter solstice and that there would be a
good harvest the following year. This tradition became linked with Christmas.

Hundreds of years ago, Christmas dinner
was very different. A popular meal was pig's
head smothered in mustard. The rich feasted
on goose, peacock or swan.

No one ate turkey until the sixteenth century, when traders brought the birds back from America. It is said that turkey became popular because King James I of England (James VI of Scotland) found it easier to digest. By Victorian times, turkey or goose were usually eaten at Christmas dinner.

Now, millions of turkeys are eaten each Christmas. They are sometimes so big that they take hours to cook – some people even put theirs in the oven on Christmas Eve!

Christmas fact

There is a tiny Y-shaped bone between the neck and the chest of the turkey. This is known as the wishbone. It is traditional for two people to pull the wishbone with their little fingers until it breaks. Whoever ends up with the biggest piece is allowed to make a secret wish.

What does 'all the trimmings' mean?

People often describe their Christmas dinner as 'turkey and all the trimmings'. Trimmings are the types of food that traditionally go with turkey at Christmas.

Roast potatoes are crunchy and delicious.

Parsnips are long, pale vegetables that are extra-tasty when they are roasted.

Stuffing is a tasty mixture of breadcrumbs, meat and spices. It can be cooked inside the turkey or in a separate dish.

Bread sauce is made by mixing breadcrumbs, milk and spices together and leaving them to bubble and thicken.

Cranberry sauce is a pinky-red sauce that is slightly sweet and slightly sharp. It goes well with turkey.

Sausages with bacon wrapped round them are a real treat!

But there's one more vital ingredient for Christmas dinner ...

Why do people eat Brussels sprouts at Christmas dinner?

Brussels sprouts are named after the city where they were first grown, hundreds of years ago – the city of Brussels in Belgium.

They are tiny cabbages that belong to the mustard family. They grow best in cooler places – there are fields and fields of them planted across Europe and the USA.

More Brussels sprouts are eaten at Christmas than at any other time of the year. Some people love them. Some people hate them. But no Christmas dinner would be complete without them.

No one knows exactly why we always eat them at Christmas. They were probably brought over from Brussels many years ago and, because they are a winter vegetable, have become a part of our traditional meal ever since.

Christmas fact
About a billion Brussels sprouts are eaten every Christmas in Ireland alone!

Why do we roast chestnuts?

Chestnuts are shiny brown nuts that grow on chestnut trees. When they are roasted, their bristly shells split open and the nut inside is cooked and ready to eat.

In cold, frosty cities during the wintertime, stallholders roasted chestnuts on street corners. A paper bag of hot chestnuts would keep your hands warm, as well as being a tasty treat. Some people still roast chestnuts today – here's how to make your own.

What you need:

> A bag of fresh chestnuts
> A non-stick tray
> An adult

What you do:

1. Heat the oven to 200°C/400°F/gas mark 6.
2. Ask your adult to cut a cross into the top of each chestnut (just like they'd prepare Brussels sprouts). This is very important – it stops the chestnuts from exploding in the oven.

3. Shake the chestnuts on to the tray and bake them in the oven for about thirty minutes.
4. Use oven gloves to take the tray out of the oven. Then, still using the oven gloves, carefully pull the bristly outer shell off a chestnut.
5. Blow on the chestnut to cool it down.
6. Blow again.
7. Very carefully, pop the chestnut into your mouth.

How tasty is that?!

Why do we crack nuts at Christmas?

Nuts are on sale all year round. They are usually sold without their shells – ready to eat. But at Christmas, something strange happens. Bags and bags of nuts appear in supermarkets everywhere – and they all have shells that need to be cracked open. Why is this?

Wooden nutcrackers were once popular Christmas presents in parts of Europe.

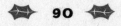

These were carved and painted to look like soldiers or kings. A nut could be cracked open in the nutcracker's jaws. Nutcrackers are now usually metal and shaped like a pair of pliers, but they do the same job. Perhaps nut-cracking is still a Christmassy activity because this is a time when people relax, sit back and simply enjoy cracking a nut or two!

A nutcracker is the star of the most festive ballet of all – *The Nutcracker*. It tells the story of a young girl called Clara who receives a gift of a Nutcracker soldier on Christmas Eve. When she falls asleep that evening, she dreams that her precious Nutcracker fights with the Mouse King. Written by Tchaikovsky, the ballet is packed with different dances and well-known music, including the 'Dance of the Sugar Plum Fairy'. For those who like ballet and Christmas, this is the perfect performance to go and see.

9

Christmas fun and games

Why do people go to see pantomimes?

There is only one reason why people go to see pantomimes – because they want to have a brilliant time. *Oh, yes they do!*

Pantomimes are plays that are performed around Christmas time. They are usually based on popular fairy tales and stories such as *Aladdin*, *Jack and the Beanstalk*, *Dick Whittington*, *Cinderella* and *Sleeping Beauty*.

Pantomimes are packed with jokes, songs and dance. But perhaps the best thing of all is that the audience is allowed to shout back at the actors. So, if you're going to a pantomime, get ready to shout ...

HE'S BEHIND YOU!   OH, NO THEY DON'T!

OH, YES THEY DO!

BOOOOOOOO!   HISSSSSS!

HURRAY!

Christmas fact
Pantomimes date back to Roman times, when a masked actor called Pantomimus performed a show of dance and mime. In the early nineteenth century, a clown called Grimaldi began many well-known traditions of pantomime.

Why does a man play the pantomime dame?

In the world of pantomime, anything is possible. The actors are louder, bolder and more dazzling than anything seen on stage for the rest of the year.

The pantomime dame is one of the most important characters. She is very funny, extra-outrageous and wears a big, brightly coloured dress, stripy tights and a huge wig. Best of all – she is played by a man! This is one of the great pantomime traditions and it may be because, hundreds of years ago, all of the characters in plays were played by men. Or it may simply be because it's really funny!

Pantomime dames aren't the only ones who get the chance to dress up as a member of the opposite sex. The leading 'boy' – such as Dick Whittington or Prince Charming – is always played by a woman.

Christmas fact
A pantomime is the only time you are allowed to shout at actors!

How do you play charades?

Charades (said *sher-rards*) is a game that is traditionally played at Christmas. The only equipment you need to play is a watch or clock that counts seconds. An egg timer would be perfect.

The aim of the game is to act out the name of a well-known film, song, book, television programme or play – without speaking!

What you do:

1. Show your audience what type of thing they are guessing. For a film, pretend to be using a film camera. For a song, pretend to be singing. For a book, pretend to open your hands as if you're opening a book. For a TV programme, draw a box with your finger. For a play, draw a set of curtains in the air. (An adult will be able to show you how to do all of these if you're stuck.)
2. Hold up one, two, three or more fingers to show your audience how many words there are in the phrase they are guessing.
3. Now act out each of those words. This is easier than it sounds. For example, here are some ideas for acting out some different words:

Sleeping – pretend to be asleep
Beauty – point to your lovely face or to something else beautiful
White – point to something else white
Christmas – point to all the Christmassy things you can see!

The winner is the person who guesses your secret phrase. Then it's their turn!

10

Dreaming of a white Christmas

Why do we dream of a white Christmas?

Snow makes things look extra-Christmassy, turning the world into a glittering, magical place. It doesn't fall every Christmas – and in some countries, it doesn't fall at all. Yet every year, many people hope that the coming Christmas will be a white one.

But even if the snowflakes don't arrive, there is still snow all around. There are snowy scenes on Christmas cards. Some people spray pretend snow on to their windows. And the tops of Christmas cakes are decorated with snowy icing.

Christmas fact
The biggest-selling Christmas song of all time is 'White Christmas'. It was recorded in 1942 by Bing Crosby, who later starred in the film of the same name. Records and CDs of 'White Christmas' have sold well over thirty million copies around the world.

Is it always cold at Christmas?

Although it is usually cold in the northern half of the world, it can be warm further south. For example, Christmas Day is right in the middle of the Australian summer. At this time of year, there is no chance of snow. Temperatures are usually higher than 30°C.

In Australia, Christmas Day isn't a time to wrap up in scarves, hats and gloves. It's a time to go swimming in the sea and barbecuing on the beach. And, because Christmas takes place near the beginning of the long summer holidays, children have another month off school after all of the turkey has been eaten.

Christmas fact
On Christmas Eve, Australian children some-times leave out a cool drink for Father Christmas. He needs something thirst-quenching after zooming about in the heat.

What's the best way to build a snowman?

If you are lucky enough to see snow at Christmas, why not build a Santa snowman?

what you do:

1. Make a snowball and then roll this around and around in the snow, making it bigger and bigger as you go. This will be the body. There's no limit to how big it can be!
2. Make another snowball, slightly smaller than the last one. This will be the head.
3. Carefully lift the smaller snowball on to the bigger one. Pack a little snow around the neck to make sure that the head doesn't move.
4. Now decorate your snowman! Pop a Santa hat on his head. Add stones for eyes, a carrot for a nose and a bendy twig for a mouth. You could even add a sack – packed with scrunched-up newspaper instead of real presents!

Christmas fact
Every single snowflake is a different shape. You can only see this when they are magnified.

11

The twelve days of Christmas

What are the twelve days of Christmas?

The twelve days of Christmas begin on 25 December and end on 5 January. According to the Christian church, this is the time between Jesus's birth and the visit of the three wise men, or three kings. The kings are said to have arrived in Bethlehem with their gifts on 6 January, which is known as Epiphany.

Some children have to be especially patient. Although Christmas is a huge celebration, this is *not* when they receive their presents.

In Spain, Mexico and many other countries, Christmas Day is a day for going to church and for visiting relatives and friends. *El día de reyes*, or Three Kings' Day, is when many children open their presents – the same day that the baby Jesus received his gifts.

Christmas fact

In Sweden and Finland it was once ruled that a person breaking the law on any of the twelve days of Christmas would receive a stiffer sentence than at any other time of the year.

What do the words in 'The Twelve Days of Christmas' song mean?

The words in 'The Twelve Days of Christmas' might sound like nonsense, but they are said to have hidden meanings.

Hundreds of years ago, it was very dangerous to be a Catholic in the UK. To keep things extra-secret, some children remembered important things about their religion using this Christmas song:

On the first day of Christmas
My true love sent to me
A partridge in a pear tree.

On the second day of Christmas
My true love sent to me
Two turtle doves
And a partridge in a pear tree.

On the third day of Christmas
My true love sent to me
Three French hens,
Two turtle doves
And a partridge in a pear tree ...

... On the twelfth day of Christmas
My true love sent to me
Twelve drummers drumming,
Eleven pipers piping,
Ten lords a-leaping,
Nine ladies dancing,
Eight maids a-milking,
Seven swans a-swimming,
Six geese a-laying,
Five golden rings,
Four calling birds,
Three French hens,
Two turtle doves
And a partridge in a pear tree!

'My true love' meant God and the gifts were
all things to do with the Catholic religion.

For example, the 'two turtle doves' were the Old and New Testaments in the Bible. 'Ten lords a-leaping' were the Ten Commandments.

What is Twelfth Night?

Twelfth Night is the evening and night of 5 January, which is the twelfth day of the Christmas period. This used to be a more important time than Christmas Day itself!

Instead of Christmas cake, Twelfth Night cakes were baked. These were rich fruit cakes with surprises inside, like Christmas puddings. If you found a bean, you were allowed to boss people around all night. If you found a twig, you were a fool.

Until the nineteenth century, many people held Twelfth Night parties. These were wild and exciting, with practical jokes galore. But Queen Victoria was not amused. She banned the celebration of Twelfth Night in the 1870s.

Christmas fact
Twelfth Night, one of William Shakespeare's most famous plays, was probably called

this because it was written to be performed on Twelfth Night.

Have you ever wished that it could be Christmas every day?

Christmas is such a magical time of year, you might wish that it happened every day. But would you really want to look at twinkling decorations all year round? Would you want to eat turkey and Brussels sprouts every single day? Some people love Christmas so much that this is exactly what they do!

The people of Latvia have a really fun tradition. They don't celebrate Christmas every day of the year, but they do celebrate on each of the twelve days of Christmas. From 25 December to 5 January, children receive presents every single day!

Christmas fact
The pop group Wizzard released the song 'I Wish It Could Be Christmas Every Day' in 1973. This is still played on the radio, the television and at parties every Christmas!

When should Christmas decorations be taken down?

Christmas is officially over on Epiphany, 6 January. This is the day that all the decorations should be taken down and put away. Many people say that it is unlucky to leave them up for any longer.

It's time to pluck the baubles off the Christmas tree, unwind the tinsel and pack up the fairy lights. It's time to put the tree back in the loft. It's also time to gather up all the Christmas cards. (Why not recycle them or save them to make an Advent calendar next year?)

But don't be too glum – in just eleven short months, it will be time to put all the decorations back up again!

12
More of your Christmas questions answered

How do you say 'Merry Christmas!' around the world?

Austria	*Frohe Weihnachten*
Czech Republic	*Vesele Vanoce*
Denmark	*Glædelig Jul*
The Netherlands	*Prettige Kerstdagen*
Finland	*Hauskaa Joulua*
France	*Joyeux Noël*
Greece	*Eftihismena christougenna*
Hungary	*Boldog Karácsonyt*
Iceland	*Gledileg Jol*
Ireland	*Nollaig Shona dhuit*
Italy	*Buon Natale*
Japan	*Merii Kurisumasu*
Norway	*Gledelig Jul*
Poland	*Wesolych Swiat*
Portugal	*Boas Festas*
Russia	*Hristos Razdajetsja*
Sweden	*God Jul*

Turkey	Mutlu Noeller
Pakistan	Bara Din Mubarrak Ho
Scotland	Nollaig chridheil huibh
Spain	Feliz Navidad
Wales	Nadolig Llawen

What happens if your birthday is on Christmas Day?

Just as any other day of the year, many people celebrate their birthday on Christmas Day. This is a very special day for a birthday. It means that you can spend the whole day with your family. And you might get two lots of presents on the same day!

Some people even get to have a second birthday in the summer, so that their friends can come to the party.

Famous author Robert Louis Stevenson's birthday was on 13 November. But one of his friends was born on Christmas Day and longed to have a different birthday. So, it is said that the author of *Treasure Island* (1883) left the friend a gift in his will – his own birthday!

Christmas fact
World-famous scientist Sir Isaac Newton
was born on Christmas Day.

What is special about Christmas Eve?

Christmas Eve is the day before Christmas
Day. It's a day when everyone starts to get
really excited, because Christmas is nearly
here. But for many countries, Christmas
Eve is the most important day of the whole
festive season.

In Mexico, some towns have a candlelit
parade on Christmas Eve. The sound of
singing and tinkling bells echoes through the
streets on their way to church.

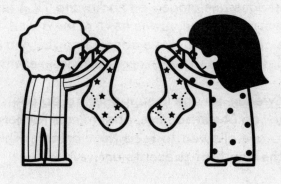

Austrian children receive their presents on Christmas Eve. It is also the first time they see the Christmas tree. When they hear the sound of a tinkling bell, they are allowed to go into a room where a dazzling tree and presents are waiting.

For people in the Czech Republic, Christmas Eve is the day when they decorate their tree. Traditionally, the only meal they eat during the day is cabbage soup. By the evening, everyone is ready for a delicious meal of fish and potato salad. Best of all, while dinner is being eaten – the presents mysteriously appear under the tree!

It's a busy day in Finland. There's rice porridge and plum fruit juice for breakfast. Then it's time to decorate the tree. Christmas messages are played on radio and TV. A huge Christmas dinner comes next. After a visit to the cemetery, to leave candles on the graves of loved ones, children receive their presents.

In Sweden, no one is supposed to do any work on Christmas Eve, apart from farmers, who are allowed to feed their animals. This is the day that presents arrive.

Why is Christmas also written as 'Xmas'?

'Xmas' is not just a modern way of shortening the word 'Christmas'. Its use can be traced back many hundreds of years.

In the Greek language, the word for 'Christ' is 'Xristos'. Five hundred years ago, Europeans first began to use the letter 'X' instead of 'Christ' in the word 'Christmas'. The tradition has stuck.

So, it is not wrong to write 'Xmas' – it's simply another way of writing 'Christmas'.

Christmas fact
The word Christmas comes from *Cristes Maesse*, early English words that mean 'Christ Mass'. (Mass is a religious ceremony. The Mass held at Christmas is one of the most important of the year.) 'Christ Mass' has now become 'Christmas'.

Has Christmas ever been cancelled?

Yes! From 1647 until about 1660, Christmas was banned by the English parliament. Oliver

Cromwell, who was in charge, was a Puritan. He was very religious and believed that Christmas should be a time for sermons and prayers. It certainly wasn't a time for celebration, when friends and family got together to have fun.

Carol singing was banned. Parties were banned. Even Christmas dinner was banned. Cromwell's soldiers snooped around the streets on Christmas Day, sniffing for the telltale smell of roasting goose. Anyone found with so much as a Brussels sprout would be punished.

Christmas trees were also outlawed – and decorations too. Oliver Cromwell even banned holly.

Aren't you glad that you didn't live in the seventeenth century!

Has Christmas Day always been a holiday?

It was only in the nineteenth century that Christmas Day became a holiday for most

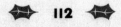

people. In many countries, Christmas Day was a day of rest, like Sundays. In 1871, it became a holiday for the whole of the UK.

In the USA, different states made Christmas Day a holiday one by one. Alabama was the first, in 1836, and Oklahoma was the last in 1907.

But not everybody gets the day off on Christmas Day. The police, fire brigade and ambulance service have to be ready for any emergencies. Hospitals have to stay open to look after patients and nurses and doctors have to be there to care for them.

It is becoming more and more popular for people to eat out on Christmas Day. Chefs cook their meals, while waiters and waitresses serve them.

And what about people who work for television companies? Newsreaders have to work on Christmas Day and camera operators have to be there to film them. However, there are very few 'live' shows on television at this time of year. Many programmes shown during the festive season are recorded before Christmas. There are also lots of films to watch. This means that most television people are free to stay at home with their families!

Christmas fact
Frank Capra's classic Christmas film *It's a Wonderful Life* was released in 1947, but did not become famous until the 1970s. It is now watched by millions of people every year.

Why is Boxing Day called Boxing Day?

No one is quite sure how Boxing Day got its name. It might have been because of alms boxes. Throughout the year, people would put money into these boxes and on 26 December the boxes were opened and the money given to the poor.

However, Boxing Day *might* be named because of servants and other employees. Servants had to work on 25 December. (After all, *someone* had to cook and serve rich people's Christmas dinner.) But, on 26 December, they were presented with a box of gifts. Best of all, they were given the day off to celebrate Christmas! Many employers still give their staff a bonus at Christmas.

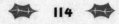

114

Do any towns and cities have Christmassy names?

Some people are reminded of Christmas all year round, because that's where they live! There's a Christmas Island in the Indian Ocean and another one in Nova Scotia, where there's also a town called Noel. There are two more towns called Noel, in Canada and in Missouri, USA.

In Florida and Arizona, there are towns called Christmas. There's also a Christmas Valley in Oregon, USA, and a Christmas Creek in Australia. In the USA, there are even towns called Santa Claus, in Arizona, Georgia and Indiana.

Christmas fact
Hollywood in Los Angeles, USA, is the home of the movie industry. It is sometimes known as Tinsel Town, not because of Christmas, but because of all the stars that live there and all the glitzy, glittering parties they go to.

Index

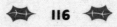

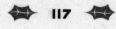